PRAISE for *DIVINE BLUE LIGHT*:

"Will Alexander is at one moment an unparalleled genius gathering psyches and sending them as grains through an hourglass. And at the next, a genius who then stills music, stills consciousness, dries consciousness for us revealing the roots of dimensionless mind. In these poems we have language in all its phases of matter; all structures agreed upon by vibrating cosmic cords... and chords of this divine blue light of which Alexander is the best gardener we have in this generation."

—**Tongo Eisen-Martin**, author of *Blood on the Fog*

"The 'invisible current' Will Alexander channels in the meteoric poems of *Divine Blue Light* is not surreal escape but vibrational engagement–an engagement with the infinite streams of the heart of being."

—**Jeffrey Yang**, author of *Line and Light*

"One of our time's most singular and prophetic poets, Alexander continues to offer his expansive and transformative vision in *Divine Blue Light*, a collection that is aptly named and resonates with the highest frequencies of wisdom, translucence, and quantum refraction. These are poems that enter your being and change the molecular makeup of existence, of vantage, of scale."

—**Janice Lee**, author of *Imagine a Death*

"As Trane, before ever receiving the primary note, had to have seared sound into sound, through sound, by the fate of neural flash accreting in a palace of blind dexterity, absent logistics of causal burden, where all creativity is honed ('poised against self-inflicting ozone assaulted while living in my crazed silo of indifference'), Will Alexander maneuvers within language that is antebreath to the invisible as improvisation ('concerning billions & billions / of curious antecedents') via birth canals of dream static. For example, I once saw Will change the weather, as easily as one might slip into a second, third, or even fourth kimono, and with a single perfect utterance. Like agua tilting itself into a god, Will's texts suffuse the horizon of Poetry with the abstract purity of their oceanic movements ('as phantoms blazing in & out of consciousness'), sun-condensing, dissolving seemingly endless sight into a disappearing instant of the Miraculous ('as if skilled interior prognostication had erupted as visible number'). *Divine Blue Light* exists by what it exudes."

—**Carlos Lara**, author of *Like Bismuth When I Enter*

PRAISE for WILL ALEXANDER:

"Since the 1980s, the Los Angeles-based Alexander has mixed politics with mesmeric, oracular lines."
—**Greg Cowles**, *The New York Times*

"A long-distance runner extraordinaire, Will Alexander parses and devours information, code and arcana lest they parse and devour him, parse and devour us. What but deep seas and distant galaxies would make such a demand his extended soliloquies implicitly ask and overtly answer."
—**Nathaniel Mackey**

"It is tempting to label Alexander a surrealist or experimentalist, but he is truly a singular voice."
—**Citation for the Jackson Poetry Prize**

"Alexander's diegesis is one of chimerical fission and transformation."
— *The Poetry Review*, London

"Alexander's verbal flights strike me as more shamanistic than free-associational or automatic. His evocation of upper and lower worlds, and his vocabulary which bridges poetry, philosophy, myth, and science, give his verbal fulgurations a sense of linguistic seed that suddenly sprouts, then resprouts... He may be the first major 'outsider artist' in American poetry. Whatever he is, he is a force to reckon with..."
—*American Poet*

DIVINE BLUE LIGHT

DIVINE BLUE LIGHT

(For John Coltrane)

Will Alexander

Pocket Poets Series : Number 63
City Lights Books | San Francisco

Library of Congress Cataloging-in-Publication Data

Names: Alexander, Will, author.
Title: Divine blue light (for John Coltrane) / Will Alexander.
Description: San Francisco : City Lights Books, 2022. | Series: Pocket
    poets series ; number 63
Identifiers: LCCN 2022011489 | ISBN 9780872868700 (paperback)
Subjects:
Classification: LCC PS3551.L357716 D58 2022 | DDC
    811/.54--dc23/eng/20220420
LC record available at https://lccn.loc.gov/2022011489

ISBN: 978-0-87286-870-0

City Lights Books are published at the City Lights Bookstore
261 Columbus Avenue, San Francisco, CA 94133.
citylights.com

CONTENTS

Preface

PREFACE

These poems remain parallel to nanograms teeming as dazzling wattage. Compared to reality as three-dimensional noun-based organization, these poems are less concerned with the palpable plane; instead the work remains sans "the tyranny of causality" kinetic via invisible current. This being current that remains un-stilled sans three-dimensional appropriation. Within my current terminology I understand this state of mind to be one of blazeless blazing not according to prior lingual aristocracy that has attempted to impose a lingual theocracy of super-imposed rationality.

—Will Alexander

DIVINE BLUE LIGHT

Condoned to Disappearance
for Fernando Pessoa

As sigil
camouflaged by curious smoke & surcease
there remains your visage enigmatic & crystal
remaining hidden
within occulted lingual ravines

at one level
it is known that your appellation
is Fernando Pessoa
born 13 June 1888
of course there exists
the perfunctory tables of your chronicle
loss of your natural father at 5
your mother's re-marriage & new placement in Durbin
then university stay
fueled by magnetic indifference then life in rented rooms
then businesses letters translated from Portuguese to English &
    French
then "criticism" written in 1912 "creative prose" in 1913
& the following year poetry
the heteronyms
their powers
their conspicuous agendas including Alberto Cairo Ricardo Reis
    Alvaro de Campos
then one brief romance

delimited publication
then death by "cirrhosis of the liver"

a "capsule"
an un-leavened symmetry
a migratory transit evinced from my written realm as co-sensation

& why do I emphasize the migratory?

is it because you've always assumed kinetics that reveal ghosts
    emerging & re-emerging from Lisbon?

Fernando
being figurative insularity
roaming a perch of invisible significance
retreating to an emblematic edge only to return as visual briefings
to emit perfection by scent
by confounding observation
lit from within by inner magnificence
your inner eye
a refracted body of diamonds
that formed as an inner cyclonics as true & concussive blood form

your poetic forces
gazing via scattered combustion understanding the rankings of
    minerals
not unlike an imaginary ostrich on fire with its primeval thesis
    understanding precursors
drafts
flowing from various forms rife with altering

your personality
human microbial filtration
as anonymous fantasmic shift of various lingual maturation
being high art as cinder
as itinerant breathing codes that range from susurrant of inaudible
    deafening

& you remained invisible
remaining silently tumultuous
not unlike a primeval calamity perhaps a burning richter as bird
    housing in your spirit
a Cryodrakan breaks
or a Quetzalcoatlus
symbolic of your oversize lingual spell
spanning your animus of heteronyms not as a gesture of looks
or feral figurines

perhaps in your case
an ashen boreal as projection that spins & declines its range not as
    cellular density
or bio-linear architecture
yet never capable of the fire of a galaxy & its range of 3 billion
    light years & counting

not as anemic arch-enemies to yourself
but heteronyms that emerge & glisten in themselves
because you understood that the void continued to blaze
as they continued to refract themselves
all the while rooted in themselves through & beyond imaginary
    compost

because the void blazes & gives strength
their psychic fracas bends & sculpts their own self-reception
so that their many personalities blazed & gave strength to living
   antonyms
to the boldness of their own psychic physique
their architecture as biography through peculiar writing climates
   they being integral burning mangers
bred to lateralize & soar within their own motion

to my understanding
none other than revealed kinetics not as the failed kinetics
of an open hearse marking time being not unlike susurrations in
   the margins
but being the Alps on fire with trans-personal imagination

your favourite motif
being charisma as the strangely nameable
suffused by surreptitious strength empowering their psyches as
   you ambled the boulevards of Lisbon
as ghost who bred molecules
via anguish & displacement
who emitted via the grand view of things

your vision cast on reasonless scraps of paper
connecting an archive of imaginary hamlets seemingly palpable
& again your principal heteronyms
Alberto Caeiro
Alvaro de Campos
Ricardo Reis
they being portion of "theatre of being"

enhanced by your amateur astrologer Raphael Baldaya
a Portuguese teacher of Zen

& de Campos a dreamer in drunkenness
floating across a windswept Lisbon as you assumed the perils of
    the itinerant

this is where you ambled the Gulf of the itinerant
not with a ruffled roar
or an entangled roar proto to schizophrenia & its warrens

not a brusque or triggered calculation
never anti-climatic
but filled with a range of luminosity that self-summoned itself &
    rose
as proliferation via consciousness far beyond entangled ideology

because the ideological self-stunts its own upheaval
via dendritic shading & blurred neurological identity
you understood the intelligence that flowed through itinerant
    mosses that evinced themselves as reasonless exhibits

tuned by marks on scraps of paper this remained your magnificent
    imaginal music
not unlike a blue & convincing x-ray according to powder
or a wheat that explores by nourishing the bladder of its future

these were your written voices that gazed
that rose & took on accents
that took on evaporated accents that rose & overtook themselves

like omens
as they continue to fertilize the future
so that riddles are formed that cleanse the neurology

your heteronyms
unlike the pseudonyms that populated Kierkegaard
not as grafts
or as strange Herculean items that rose from fundamental
   observation they had a compound complex fate as juggled
   fertility as amalgam

to literally script your 70 plus personalities
would do nothing other
than haunt the rites of ellipsis
with linear protocol & error
with bounded clinical judgment
so that hailstones & miracles
would cease to conscript their own dissemination

so instead
I realize your mind
as ceaseless with activation
never akin to acrimonious spillage somehow summoned from
   disaster & retreat

I can only feel your imaginary scalpel
as higher gain by being
of its mesmerizing willows

both swaying & flying
via a holographic sonics that blazes

it infects the multiple via the uncountable
so that it spins & merges & rises higher than the plane that
    describes concatenation
that rises higher than the fervour of ascent that kindled ideology

say a gorge & you fill it with amplification
are primeval glasses invigorated?
do they continue to vigour according to the tenets of Ernst Mach?

to you Fernando all tenets interacted & kinetics remained oceanic
because at present you survive the particle that was yourself
where lingual ravine opens lingual ravine
where nuance quickens & magically suspends itself
not according to theory imposed by obsolescence

because your script could never collapse into brazen gain
into multicellular dissection
your moods improperly quoted according to quickness & silence
    according to animation
that rendered the moment

this was poetic infiltration according to the sound of anonymous
    hives
according to the sonics of your character

for you lingual quarantine was invaded by secrecy conjured by the
routine that was Lisbon
with its grand anonymous metrics channeling their way into your
anonymous secondary realms
at times overshadowed by vernacular script

unlike its tenets you've seemed to vanish & ascend
not unlike a realm condoned to disappearance

Gargantuan Origination: Inscription
for the Collages of Dean Smith

Sandstone
carved by elements prone to the Tetheys Sea
as they carved exploded & asphyxiated
alive with water that both burned & etched
as primordium
that exploded
that dictated itself
via primordial grammes
to what seems via delimited view
Luciferean & unruly
carving minerals & minerals of rock as hallucinated grammar via a
    mysteriously distant sea
not via its form that presently exists but of record as its own
    eruption
its velocity carving primordial mineral fire
that oxygenates as propulsion enriching its own anterior element
    not as judgmental raiment or as legible sketching
but explosion sans human origination
sans seeming civilized protraction not as needle that sculpts
    according to precise human episode but as anterior trance
    projected
before its power was projected

but explosive
elemental
predating the minerals of sharks anterior to their own explosion as
    waste

thus
rocks are carved by the dialectics of salt
flowing as power
that mimics the mystical

thus water
accrues as the mystical
carving spontaneous hieroglyphics not as burdensome sand
but power that engulfs & self-strategizes itself

as it implies other maelstroms
that pre-date themselves
that burn beyond local stellar orientation
knowing in themselves markings that cascade from anterior
    galactic spells sans illusion that grips fixation

& this grammatical water
not prelude to something other than itself
yet always implying subsequent impalpability
not unlike the stirring of galaxies that loop via gargantuan
    origination

A Blaze of Riddles

Because the Sun exudes a blaze of riddles
there exists a haze of optimal osmosis
of protracted helium that bends
via its forceless gruel
via its maniacal translocation
to alien ravines
to other planes & possibilities anterior to the sense of chronicle as
    uninhabited or pure activity

Ravenous Spectral Pores

By exercising
cryptic tales of ponies & harems
I distract
from whatever cause is pouring
vis à vis necessitous solar inferno as mirrors reflect one's ravenous
    spectral pores
that condense as a summary form of glass
so should I wander across its sums
I understand that my speculation issues from tornadic rivers
from ice-hot temperatures
so that I am both sans & simultaneous
concerning billions & billions
of curious antecedents

Oneiric Liminal Memo

Facing terse argumentative neural confrontation
poised against self-inflicting ozone assaulted while living in my
    crazed silo of indifference
knowing its void to be magically elevated
as resonant chimera
as if fire were to erupt
from sub-consistent mountain ranges
as erring
fabulous
knowing my figment
to be nothing nothing other than transactional scintillation

In a Pitch Dark Sailing House

Vertiginous
in a pitch dark sailing house
as alienated spinning figment
I ambulate as galling paper road
as phantoms blazing in & out of consciousness
as otherness
as alienated other
peering down on myself
from a coeval sky
facing a scale that enters ashes
as a chronicle of non-sequiturs being rays from Saturnian winds
    because there exists nothing except nothing I can squander
nothing that curious bookcases brew
so that fire appears from urns
as if it were a territorial omen
as electrocuted scar
alive
as magical utterance
as roughage self-specified in opening form onto random scholarly
    dust
thus
asking myself the one-line equation of how astonishment boils

Re-Extolling Barbarism

While feasting from a table scattered with worms & millet
I am thinking of astigmatism
blasphemous
staggered by nullification & grafting by methods rife with a
    sojourn of blizzards
so that a dark & carnivorous testing path occurs
scripting a journal of spells according to unsparing density
    according to the sonics of transparency
according to microbe warrens left as interior forms of evidence
    perhaps sounds from bodiless Martian ravines
perhaps a deafening colloquy by quarrel

Neo-Rulership

Within my plaintive spectral condition
neo-rulership corresponds to asymmetrical creeping
to strange tautological curses
to strange oblivious strata modelled by quality
being none other than scholarship configured out of mayhem
as if one listened to an eclipsed saurian curiously laying gelatinous
    scorpions' eggs
believing itself to be anterior quality magically sculpted out of
    nothingness
from ignited stationary drift
as if power from garroulous drainage had turned coding against
    itself
as if skilled interior prognostication had erupted as visible number
    being forces of degree by counting
this is when the nerves erupt as beacons beyond the sieve that is
    calibration
sans the epistemological as scale or referential ideation
burgeoning as cartographic plenums

A Series of Sub-Particulates

A blur leaping out of sleep awakened while riding a solemn
    methane pony

Vascular ravens
flying through predatory substrates

Sudden Cambodian flares
not unlike a leakage of diamonds

Ruined plasma
as new & menacing sea forms on Saturn

Prayer being energy that burns
as quest for magical evidence of itself

The modern world
a constant migration towards unhappiness & seclusion

An infestation that swelters

Anterior Cartography

Certain wavelengths appear
not as beatific summation
but as feral anterior cartography where terror attempts to invade
   our interior translucency

translucence being magical
being evolutionary lightning
being a curious spinning of drought & transparency
that rises up from opposites
so incapability seemingly transpires where maimed grasses contort
   as untreated saliva
the latter being of spiraling truncation
of oblique & dazzling darkness
possessing epileptic strength that is awkward & improvident
as if the Sun had erupted & gone ill

according to higher rotational degree
Í am able to view this first spoiled leakage
from clarified detritus
from splintered metrics & sand

so how does seeming drought silently erupt & explore itself?

perhaps as a mis-focused cataract filled with dimming ocean parts
   with nervous topiary eels
akin to negated asparagus rooting

thus
result as botched uranium entanglement
as flummoxed escalation
with general visage of characterological explanation creating
    animated rifts along the equator of the Nile

under this condition can we say that the moon blazes from a cold
    & rigorous coffin
from a despicable but dis-claiming that illuminates refractive
    properties from hell?

perhaps I remain an in-human courier from Draco
from in-celibate wastes
where proto-carrion feed
via unveiled obscurity that seems to not exist
where a phylum of tar is struck by un-impeachable lightning
that irrevocably pre-exists & becomes green and green-black

this being chemistry
that has extolled itself as if seeing itself on a galleon of waters
guided by pre-imagined birds
by a syllabus prior to a cartography of rainbows

so how does this quell evil attacking organic wetlands?

one must persist in altering one's view
as sub-atomic mimic
allowing to view the gist
that is European capital
with its dark vehicular thirst

with its blinded mechanical pieces tragically testing measurement
it remains none other than a serpent of cataracts
of doomed & fore-shortened brain stems
allowing one to see
fiendish ghosts
riled anathema ponies
that rotate as notation according to evil as famished consequence
according to stain as it secretes as a kind of negligible quanta
according to Dark sub-quanta & its variants

this is where ignition rivals itself
by fostering inclemency as blackness
as thriving tendency that graces collective identity with jaundiced
    ability
to ruin
to cast about as fate
conjoined to the skeletal negation of itself

& we know this level of option to be carnivorous
to be Salamandrine & opaque
akin to body according to brutish seizure
seemingly porous to malevolent instigation

because such culture remains sordid
not unlike congested flocks of vapour
cast in historical daylight

thus
natural cycles swarmed by exhaustion
via heretical investigation as trans-suggestive forces

because the zodiac has been transmuted
not vanquished & squandered away on a sub-liminal isle
where the mind can never explore itself or bear power according
   to medicinal enrapturement
according to medicinal listening as exposure

hence
suppression has cast its lot upon our neurological realm
& so it appears that the hieratic has tilted allowing other
   conditions to combine
& they inscrutably rise above telepathic claustrophobia
as shifts in one's signaling that transpire & re-combine
according to the deftness of dice & anathema
as protected combinatorial combustion
so that perhaps an Oryx speeding through a wetland will furtively
   amaze itself
via its chronically imposed cellular limit weaving in & out of itself
   so that it alchemically transmutes eternity

Anterior Speculation

Imagination equates with anterior speculation. In the higher states one need not embrangle oneself via super-imposed reductive oscillation. Should skills persist at this level, if they become capable of bringing into view alchemical scars that seemingly hamper or renew samsara, an ambling evinces itself via Indigenous understanding, being praxis that magically emanates and heightens the zero field.

Phantom Inter-Dimensional Activity

Dining upon a phantom Inter-Dimensional blood yield
I remain then a barricaded wolf suspended inside a culture of
    phantoms
so as to reap strange articulation from Sulphur
I see all of the above as a glossary of rays floating in & out of one's
    optic canals
so as to peer beyond the caliginous via inverse ferment
as proactive calliope
that insists on startling & consequential contour
so higher emptiness concurs
not unlike a rhetoric that swarms with declivitous capacity
having an explosively strange assessment of itself

Transitional Sub-Weavings

The cell as micro-architectural kinetics
as an articulation of glass
spun as circular transition
at base
being bio-conundrum as nutation
akin to astonished ringing

Bodies that have erupted from the field
via random electro-chemical charge
have not failed as energy
or implausible drafts
but function in the realm of bio-chemical concussives
evolved from elusive isolation
from random pre-Cambrian explosion

Mathematical symmetry
alive as blinding electrical phasma

The body as primordial tenet
as part of the Archean era exploding
parallel as to prokaryotes & quaking

Mountainous electrical ballet
as strange angular reception
as perfect seismic amplification

Post-Fukushima
the species currently coheres
as seismic vibrational wandering

Body as application of drought
as ferocious micro-chemical flare

The physics of alien signs that tends to procure in its wake perfect
primeval kindling

Base circulation as crater always sensing its own abandonment as
grammar

Physics that magically challenges itself as strange pre-operant
beast.

Cryodrakon
seemingly self-bred as obscure pterosaur
77 million años ago
present & hauntingly prior to itself
feasting on lizards & mammals
alive via 10-meter wing span
collectively aligned with Azhdarchids

Potassium as mystical dioxide
as protracted glandular upheaval

The African psyche
that self-constructs itself as circularity by rhizome
by seminal flux
unlike super-imposed topiary weaving

The Raven as Incantatory Nuclei

As an invisible tri-unial spell
that parallels as crucial invisible species
not as outward glow or movement or techniques that console as
    frottage
but as inward alacrity
not as mechanism
as a consoling blue raven yet it vanishes into a random chronicle
    into billionths & billionths of tonality as consciousness
& dissolves & rises as momentary habitation
never at the scale that evinces as noun-based palpability
but presence sans pattern as palpability
without winged industry that engulfs its own mirage
not philosophical claustrophobia
or conscripted in-souciance
but as Planck current
sans symbolic leprosy rate
because it flies not as dazed religious beacon
no longer symbolic of embrangled chariots carving their own
    distance through self-proclaimed inferno
but as un-colored quarks & kinetics as bottomless mass
as sub-atomic proton thesis
as simultaneous blue light
as curious sapphire foundry burning
majestic
within the predatory realms
of its own incantatory nucleii

Peripheral Terminology

Not having imbibed Ghosts or dust or forces that condone
    objective termination
I remain as peripheral terminology not unlike the paradoxical
    sweltering
that erupts from one's grasp
pre-cellular in origin

Fragment: Blaze as Unknowable Drift

Blaze as unknowable drift
as mathematical drift that blazes with ciphers
I've listened to moons eclectically rise
to conundrums blaze & ascend
not as molecules
or distributed torrents
but as vibrational mazes
as curious oneiric cartography

Original Language

As a blizzard of birds
as Hottentots
as density by phonemes

Borderless Hypotactic

Not strategic salvo by mass
or ultra sonic compendium as confine
but simultaneity alive
as unpredictable dys-function
akin to itself as borderless hypotactic

Divine Blue Light: Sudden Ungraspable Nomadics
for John Coltrane

Not as phantom blinding
but the soils of Mount Meru
as quantum
as perpetual
as Inter-Dimensional kindling

its hemispheres colliding
as bricolage
as osmosis
as sonic notation
alive as sonic cometary phantoms understood unto themselves as
    stratospheric particulates
not merely as tense foundational structures
as a pronoun to be levied as simple sonic ramification

you understood this to be in the infinity of your heart
to be microscopic musical grammar
not unlike phosphates
as a syntax of symmetry resounding as an obverse mirroring of
    chords

analogous to 16th notes
rising & scattering of their own accord
much like the residue from diamonds that bake
not simply shrill supplication as noise
but as spectral realms of themselves

being sonic blinding bodies
that rise & loop & gather themselves on the other side of
    themselves
not as artefact or translated merger but as exploration summons
so that the sonic never wizens by pursuing entangled osmosis
as complex utopian turquoise

& it was on this plane that you & Dolphy squared private
    comment into thrilling electrical prophecy that both forged &
    scrambled light
so that amperage split apart & scattered
across soil as interregnum
being blizzards of grammar
not merely emitted from bodies
but sound as hail from unknown wizardry as that sired sonic
    thoughts & streams
understanding such flow as transmuted acre

can such emit itself from sounding boards of dust never
    attempting to lean on criminal piety
all the while ignited by sonic invisibility
as sub-divided notation
as darkened gradient
as chain reaction

Coltrane
this evokes its merit
as spontaneous rotation
& from your collective eye
a spontaneous emission of notes as you both assembled

the once constructed Delilah

its fragile figurines ignited
as from curious poles on Saturn being ionized rotations spun from
    Rasheed Ali
beckoning motifs from light
from minuses of hail
that emit from themselves anecdotal grammar

I am thinking of your sound alive as chronic pre-character
as limitless pre-clusters & fragments

as sonic & parallel to themselves as functioning domain as rhythm
being astral space sired as simultaneous visions of itself

I think of the songbook that was Disney
its apparitional proportion
via chronic disappearance that reappears
& spins its own subversion of itself

not merely terrestrial subset of itself
of its anguish & its motives
aligned to rhetoric that blindsided & lifts as former body by
    vibration other than the anguished motives that attempt to leap
    from protracted sterility

Trane
not merely the vibrational suffix of a monk
your fuel of darting measures
your approaches to Harmony remained creatively self-suspended

this remains your nebulous aquamarine
your inspirational aquamarine parallel & brazen with your own
    self-abandonment
an insurrection
self-fused by higher rendering as darkened guidance
with your old intestinal ferment as silence

this being the range that advances itself to yourself

so sonic memorization by line
by concrete measure to itself will always migrate
will ferociously outstrip the singular line

thus ignited wholes broken into fragments
not parallel as threnodies
but as simultaneous summons of themselves
magnetized
self-guided by bricolage
by grammars that incite arousal

not garrison according to linear ambush
but ferment grace
the ferment that embrangles grace with all its improbable
    complexity

thus linkage
as concussive charisma
as shadowy spirals
as exploded suns

create densities of themselves
being spirals whirling as interstellar omniscience
being sonic bursts
being scribbled calibrations naturally understood as sonic
   conduction

Trane
you explored the sonic combustion of mirrors
their pillaged after-count
the wilderness of grace that they found in themselves
not as iconographic shedding
or a form
a form of bewildered dust masquerading as cornucopia by fraction
that ignites its own darkening
that heightens & inscribes its own maiming

with Elvin
you formed a glare
that shielded your soul from great wresting
as you rose from invisible tombs formed from strange asteroidal
   formations

perhaps
when speaking to Dolphy & Elvin you convened as a tribe of
   cellular Gods
by eluding all cellular approach
& become vacant

mesmerized by this vacancy
the feral rose & energized its own option
sans tactical mists & pre-cognitive carbon
perhaps I can feel your shapes as murals of glass burning
forging themselves via opposing agendas
with sound reflected from invisible yields from the body

knowing that free access thrives between stars
your energy continues to bloom throughout invisible notation

the latter alive
as ungraspable sonics
not unlike the music of Herons

thus I understand your exploded constellations
their breeched tendencies
that breeched vestiges
as neutron array
as mesmerizing twilight
so that principle minuses remain broached
not as simple dialectical osmosis but as peculiar free exchange with
    essence
beyond the throes of post-manipulation
always leaping tendency as non-limit

never a brokered treatise
or a hail that limits itself through envy
but molecules that subsist & dazzle
as embittered wonderment
as cratered testaments & inscriptions

this being the realm by which suns emerge & spin

as Ernst Mach put it
this being the manner by which gestures move suns
this being the manner by which hands elongate & spill around
    corners

this being quantum power
as it increases subsistence on a cognizant plane
as a kind of theoretical groping
yielding candela by emptiness
alive as pointless micro-hectares
being analogous to heat sans a high trail of deserts
akin to toneless micro-calling
not unlike an owl
addressing its sound to unsustainable rubies

alive
as quantum testament to its fever
to its realm of microbial sub-states

thus
I hear the mesmerizing waltz of Chim Chim Cheree
& the hypnotic parallels of itself as cartographical phantom
being sub-consistent with its own field of broken micro-
    boundaries
being witness to its own unsettling

& your mind John
being simultaneous & unsettling

never as link to mystical typical personal secrecy your post-body
osmotically grappling with a chronic phantom wall
not vertical retreat into supreme cosmic expanse

as if your phantom dioxide
could be called silver
as it blends with expanded heliopause

where power evinces the limitlessness
the arcane appellation of itself
thus ceasing at gross or dictated boundaries
issuing from your field a series of infinites
that sonically ascend through themselves
not unlike ascending the sheer "Shark" wall of Mount Meru
giving a blinding lecture to itself
mesmerically set afloat within the wisdom of its own
    entanglement

but route as quantum lettering that flourishes by bizarre dictation
by highest disregard for perusal by fragmentation
thus the impersonal ignites as divine blue light
as bizarre philosophical gesture
analogous on Earth to unclaimed trenches
where perhaps
imaginary owl fish invade their own borders
suddenly disappearing into transmuted lightning

John
these are realms where the mind fails to match itself
as it magically intertwines with its own generating harvest

always alive
as phantom
as prophecy

as if a voice had pillaged a transparent kiosk
& divided its own cast of molecules
quintessential
never chronically harried or questioning its own canonical fluidity

Trane
it was your sonic grammar that climbed
& now registers as sonic echo far beyond gregarious misnomer
not as dazed mercurial haunting
or as plague
or as sound that roams as superstitious poltergeist
but as anthem of itself
as profound philosophical altering of itself

as if lesions were controlled amidst their own self-dissemination
being spontaneous paradigm that guides itself throughout galaxy
    after galaxy
not simply
as electromagnetic conundrum
but as confoundment
as philosophical weltering of itself

the profundity of paradigm
your increased nature via ascent
always guiding itself via phosphenes as symbols

of sonic rhetoric
of inscrutable sonics

& these symbols hover & increase their own electricity
as curious electrical charisma
as gnostic tutoring of themselves
listening to vapour electrically extending itself
not as quotidian measurement
but as suns that extend & measure themselves
never confined to the testament that is reason
but as curious solar element
not as barren niche
or relativistic compound
but as the highest drama that specifies complexity

Human Presence That Lingers as Distorted Molecule

Present human scale
weighed as micro-carbon
as suffix
as dazzling suffocation of itself

alive as stifled mystery
as collapsed tourniquet that expands rancour in its mind
that tends to scavenge its own mystery arrayed in scab-riddled
    dressing gowns being procreated glamour as self-spawned debility

this being cradle as disabled identity
as a wilderness of mirrors
its mind slowly spinning in tandem with a ferris wheel of razors
pained
self-chronicled inside its own self-suspended dice of euro-
    occidental dilemmas
that self-instills corrupted linearity
that retains as its power slivers of torment that remains unto itself
    dazzled fractionation

thus garish fascination constantly lingers from inert stirring at
    birth to the grave beholden to simulation
to captured fatigue
tending to procreate distraction as neo-renewal
being claustrophobia as insight
stunted within splendiferous reduction

psychic maturity akin to owls that protractedly moan
rendering the same enunciated vowel sound
as strategy through language

therefore
its central expression diluted
its lingual astronomy goaded by reduction
its nerve ends deluded by barrenness
by repetitious study of itself
condoned to brazen static
to foreshortened impairment of itself

thus a phantom electric nerve yield
a lessened procreational nerve yield corrupted by tense statistical
    phantom grammar
that potentially yields a solar force 25 trillion miles from our
    momentary continents
being micro-yield of our disfigured journey

thus
a matrix of lepers
scorned by self-revulsion of themselves

According to Stellar Scale
for Sian Proctor

Stellar scale
risen above wizened technical complexity synonymous with a
    carriage of moons being vapour
that rises & electrifies the cells according to true interior
    functioning
according to voltage that submerged itself while soaring
according to balance as magnetic heightening
not as extension harassed behind a wall of borders
but magnetism as ignited significance
that partakes of parsecs
that inspires revelation
being ignited first health
where being conjoins with itself as aboriginal revelation

Nervous Incomparable Dictation

Blackness as co-equal with blackness siring initial seismicity through which initial balance is shifted ignited beyond its prior capacity so that prior balance can only gift itself by means of vertiginous causality, by seeming ruin that never instigates demise, but opens onto a primordial plane sans replication such as dates and names and habits. Nouns in this state remain posited and alit according to one's private scale that registers Greco-Roman diminishment incapable of solar vastitude. Its carnal informational complexity mired in ongoing seclusion, narrowed by its compulsion towards blinding. Being incompatible with internal states of athletic crystallography, thus blackness blazes and bends analogous to incorruptible molten.

Yet such a process of variability needs sustain itself at a pitch of strenuous characterological performance that understands itself as other than transactional value, as other than transactional crafting. For want of a better term such craft condenses to transactional lucre. What seems most called for is a counter-rotational grammar that allows internal scale to spin via intuitive heightening. This being surreptitious motion as cellular bucolic, for instance, motion across a cellular acorn delta, or perhaps, a greenish mountain sea, diabolically connected to a feral mountain climate understood to be failed mammalian gardening that curiously posits transit to alternate fables of quantum mammalian renewal superseding itself as circumvented hamlet consumed by poisonous asters oddly placed not unlike a replicated fever.

This being language as spontaneous current, as primordial electrification self-removed from private exteriority that burdens and provokes perpetual lingual ailment. This being not unlike psychic integument alive as dazzling germination, as ghostly gestural diary as written expression becomes an anti-clerical property sans phonemic claustrophobia. Thus it enacts itself as beauty via blurring, as dynamic via quickened verbal crimson. I understand this state to be one of cosmic amplification, proto-elliptical as narration flashing prior to its own existence, being a postulate of its own inclement carbon so that an evolved verbalics transpires and emits from itself something staggered and spontaneous not unlike an inferno of mist that subsumes its own charisma. During this prestigitated aural transmission I encounter a counterclockwise inferno with its powers tending to infer powers not unlike those of pre-existence. Powers prone to the inevitable mystery that remains pre-existence.

I think of powers co-equal to those of giant sunfish magically basking, gazing back at themselves igniting a phantom posthumous largesse. Of course they speak to themselves via fleeting endemic parallels that mirror magical meta-existences. These existences being a combination of spectrums simultaneous with alchemical impact alive as imperceptible planes drawing on themselves alive as impalpable lingual blazing. An invisible gust akin to self-fomented seepage pre-bodiless within this level of context. A bodiless heritage akin to phantoms striding as phantom Bedouin combinations. Combinations never negated via motionless inference, the latter scale never reflecting the noun-like scale that reflects a delimited zodiac.

This being an unconditional conundrum that by its nature seems forceless according to static empirical utterance. Of course this latter condition can now be uttered as aural example that issues its power via insistent canonical figments. These figments being quantum in nature explode through fragments that regather themselves as lateral apperception that naturally re-harvest themselves according to improbable blankness. This being ageless aural ascent up feverish astral summits. This being dictation that lends itself to the ungraspable, to what I gather to be a pluperfect sonics, not unlike a spell that continues to listen to itself thriving via vibrational independence.

Accessing Gertrude Bell

Should I isolate your brilliance
by pausing its causation
as if you were an artefact
or a scorched round shell
I could never name you
as seminal tactician
or queen mistress of hives

I would render your scale
one of cryptic molecules
that existed according to causality by debacle

your war diplomacy
led to friction
to pre-cloned attempts at utopia
but always your raw unaided colonizer's postings
summoned from inherent manoeuvring
& your mappings
alive with pre-cloned attempts at utopia
alive with the holocausts to follow

you
as lone wolf
as primeval with guile
as ignited & imperative with fortitude

as mapmaker
bifurcating desert terrain
as spy insistently indicating names
who graced the region with foreshortened compassion
complexifacation being your orbit as danger
with its obligation to decipher

the longstanding secrets
the lingual powers of the tribal wives
who clarified deficits
who understood your activity as glassy incremental flux

being subdivided with Lawrence in the Arab bureau
casting ripples that ignited future life & death
not as omnipotence
but strategy as colonial conformity

because you ignited the blazing archaeology of mapping as
    transmission
future death was summoned
a cheereless residue was defined
Faisel ibn Hussein
a brokered monarch
understood principle aspects of your tremor

thus
the void you instilled
hastened volatility
always subsumed within your demeanour

Sans Phantom Neurotic Yield

Because phenomena post-exists itself
it is incapable of induction
of deferring its nexus as nouns
cleaving to their post-remains
or worlds unto themselves like phantom moons
adrift
without suns
sub-solar in essence
not unlike sonic electrons
sans phantom neurotic yield

Grammars from Other Suns

The human state as negated micro-torrent
never alive as flux
sans dialectical originality
masquerading as subatomic particle as noun
a blinded equation unto itself
that can't portend livingness as transmuted range
as incendiary compass field
that fuses riddles
that accelerates mystery
that spirals as the field engaging the 8th chakra
as sub-blended quantum nuance
that enlivens its partial power beyond itself as compound stasis
as episodic gesture
its plenum never absorbing grammars from other suns

Mantric Blizzard as Space

A continent
that has made a covenant with its own ruin
has made the skies starved
has made stone momentarily disadvantage itself

Its circumstance deeper than tremors remains equational habit
    miming itself
via counted tablets of time

not a mantric blizzard of space into empty air
but every piece of ice as mathematical symbol

not a living quotient
but a dazed nutrient gone awry

a dark veering
stumbling over its own loins

& because
I am at nerves' end
I can only breathe mantras
& live within

Darkened Solar Implication

Lunar signals on Earth
being a sign of splotched deficits
deficits that are ashen
prone to protracted psychological cholera

so as seas rise
blindness builds as vertiginous nostrums
as blizzard by analysis
being corpse by rising corpse

mathematics alive according to protracted weather
yet rise of the seas as monumental assault
never assessed in terms of tonnage of gallons
in terms of inundated harbors
flooded spill ports.
or any other grasp of the land

this disfigured moon as sign
as splotched aerial aerial configuration
as living nightmare chalice
as if all composed water had lost its tension
perfectly predicted by living indigenous count

I am thinking of the hand as fractionation
so to ascend beyond drawn estimate
creating in its wake
darkened solar implication

being invisible refugee in Arnhem Land
being alive far beyond counted scale as timber
beyond corresponding human desolation

Language: Replete with Transformative Monsters

Language
as scaled erisma
as amplification that burns
& activates its own neter or principle
that blazes via written skill or utterance
& sonically blinds with its own display

then at times it ignites architectural imbalance
never leavened or counted as enabling distraction
but as ghost that sullies its own mirrors
that scripts itself as blazing micro-wheel
as insecticidal pattern that blurs
that dispels its own leavening
being contradiction that irrigates milk & salt

aligned with temperature
that leaps its own invasion of itself
so that it multiplies & insults the stillness of precursive rational
    stillness
& positively insults endemic rational linearity
rational linearity that attempts to cleanse its own nightmare
in the form of dialectical of prognostification
that all the while falsifies poetic current

this falsification attempts to raise & re-drown all that is living

indeed
poetic current
not as inordinate savagery
but as refined alchemical emblem
as flow that annuls inherent carbon as fatigue

for instance
white heat as helium
that forms a trellis of green mazes
instinctive with alacrity that is molten

transitional as perfection
as ignited cerulean spindle
as great white kelp that originates its own spinning
what I understand to be uranian counter-flow
gurgling within the wrath of its own shimmer
the opposite of Venusian deltas
rising as swans self-converging with themselves
as perfectly condensed arteries prior to alienation
not as static ruin or non-essential rambling but alive as phonemic
    density
sans cognitive doctrine
but as owls landing on curves
that remain alive as aleatoric octaves
in the forefront of themselves
as if they were caves leaping from themselves
being spectral sedition
alive as phonemic immediacy
beyond strange concussive calculation

an immaculate conception of itself
an incalculable frequency
as if waters could bend as an operant magical steel
as echo
as transfigured astonishment
perhaps as blank electrical moons
beyond catastrophe trapped within an inoperable pluvial setting
perhaps a gathering volcano of moons
that exists as a wind-blown monicker or a dazzled bulletin or a
    graph
beyond the state that erupts as in-grown engrown engagement
    with simmering hallucination beyond the percolation of
    coelacanths
all in the name of suspended spell

according to micro-alignment
with its ghosts
its journeys
its spirals
its coruscating condition as matter
as maze that fundamentally scatters itself
as quantum internality
that further kindles its own spirit
parallel to solar fire
being alterity that beckons

not as subsequent vehicular habit
but as a form of dawn that re-inhabits itself
as seeming mystical commencement
being a rising arc of light

being triangles bending
as shapes that no longer fatigue themselves

being blue arcana as mystery that mesmerizes itself
& confronts its own entangling
so that it embraces itself as anti-tautology
as spring that glistens
via anachronistic nerve ends
that then spirals & fails its own conclusion

as if the Sun were a new red star shining
on an ice-strewn blackness
alive as a feral of optimum engaging itself
that optimizes strange infernos of itself

so its spells rise foretell themselves
according to blackened coloration
dispelling its own disharmony

not flotational ozone that reflects
its own static burial pattern
but remains bat-like
ungrafted
not as optimal saffron
or coveted wind via conversational motive

language not assembled embitterment
or ruse
or disjunctive gesture
but alive

peering into itself
as honed emblem
replete with transformative monsters

The Mind as Quantum Quintessence

What remains as standard optical sight remains replete with non-
    tremor
stunted by psychological opacity
that remains clinical
quantifiable only capable of prior mention yet as leap
becomes tremulous with undermined inertia
as it starts to fulfill the helium in its clauses being profundity
    within its own self-dissension
a mirage
a phantom frequency
that magically shifts glowing with its own momentum
open & alive
prone to acceleration
to sub-range
to micro-tendency
tense with weighted fertilization
yet as tendency
prior to measurable synapse or pulse
proto to ungovernable bulletin or pulse
not pulsation as ineptitude
as I peer into my inner lens
I sense the tone of inevitable molecules
that occur before they occur
not as relic that ignites its own hounding
so it infuses its own oneirics

never as infected resonance
but as incandescence that blurs
always sensing palpable meta-ranges

Ghostly Bonding by Kinetic

Since the living body persists
as strange accelerated crimson
what of its post-biology through ideas through ghostly bonding
    with itself as kinetic?

does it persist within its after-state via chewn reindeer?

or does it unearth itself via post-mortem figment?

because kinetics reabsorb themselves
they remain trenchant
as certain owls
roaming the horizon as signs

Nervous Electrical Compounding

Say
the nerve ends glisten
as stark neuronal turquoise
not as nervous hatchery
but as evolutive emblem hatching via proto-memory
prior to the wastes of the Cambrian electrification
unleashing being
being mystery as the soilless body
reaching back to non-existent amplification compounded as
    proto-statistic that remains uncountable
as hallucinatory proto-body
unleashing being as its own being
its channel alive as electrical compounding
as spurious trilogies
as spur to the unknown
as possible horseshoe crab
being curious electrical hatchery
before the drought of ideology as discipline
the latter we know as nerves according to civil compunction
not rival oblong statute
or claim as summoned ambrosia
being dazed human alacrity
yet I'm thinking of bursts as patterns
not in a prone or optical sense
but in the manner that starfish ignite their crescents as neon

Deficits: Chaïm Soutine & Joan Miró

Earlier on
negatively imprisoned by chronic familial assessment
Miró
as if anonymous crime had been proposed a misdemeanor linked
    to Teutonic deficit
to bleak & conjoined unfurling
a chronicle devoid of light as efficiency essence implanted as
    perpetual doubt judged
by the projected field of others
you were a dense mystagogic trampoline according to contorted
    attempt

as for Soutine
embittered
within a rural world of murder
a combustion of nerves
of gestures condoned by nervous conquering statics
absorbing chronic social signals by non-sequitur

Under Corporate Worship

Sunday
being elliptically feigned
tautological circumference

Hierarchy as Oblivion

The quantum plane subjected
prone to detraction
to seeming assets chronicled as cognitive anomaly
to noun-based pronation
chronicled as asset more favourable to stasis
to noun-enhanced summation embrangled by measurement
by cloud according to centimeter
so activity is deigned as palpably significant
bound in greater degree by static pattern
according to recorded grammar
according to primary scale of genetic dystopia
more radical than the compounded fragment

quanta being more than fertile stationary drift
being no more than additive summation
revealed via chronic limitation as absence
conveying more
than simple refraction or mist

this conveys nothing other than tautology trapped within itself
alchemically deformed & scrambled
within itself as hierarchy
as oblivion

The Death Support System

According to enforced ideological fissure
there exists no tenor or background
that lends itself to the future

because it projects its stunted hive as emblem
its mud boils
its symbols turn brazen
it projects itself as stunted model
as vilified continuum

its captaincy
claims its power through mazes
through fatigue
through misappropriated conjunction

Inner Palpability

Implied inner palpability as transpersonal dictation
all works composed as a musical ark
as if rowing in an isthmus of lightning

the threat through rising vapour currents
hissing with dissolution

this being none other than internal cartography
ghostly cipher as interiority by number
again ghostly flares & ciphers as if the arc from lunar suns had
    risen

therefore suns appearing above suns
ignited via the blue fragmentation that is grace

The Alchemical Androgyne

As our species strides into blank electrical gulfs
we begin to possess a power
that magically subsumes & expels recto-linear chastisement
as gesture
as empirical summons
as electrification by blockage

Hierarchical Lightning

Hierarchical Lightning
being sudden optical sums
diffuse with pointillism
where one seems seismically de-enlivened not unlike a host of
    spells
extending as the 8th chakra
simultaneous with interior rhyme

this being a strange migrational hamlet
as a cluster of suns rising into observed electron space
as invisible electrification

perhaps as glow from dark springtimes
by nerves at the cusp of physical limits
this being the highest mode of aspiration
the 8th chakra blazing as transmuted limbic system

sans the borders of nightmares

sans oneself as detestable unit
as scorched melancholia
as active with sidelong glance sans formation by clepsydra

this can never form as mastery by sum
or chronicled hive
at the penultimate side of vapour as mortality

sans quinine formation

sans perfect electron crossings

sans all capabilities measured via darkened waste

therefore an isometric barrier
a sudden branch of quelling
this being a fabulous dearth that drifts in & out of salt
not unlike linear boundaries transmuted by the Oort dimension

so all prior limitation seems to linger in itself
disappearing as exploded cadence

this being energy as quantum spectrum
as phantom habitat
that roams within itself ad-infinitum

this being speech that aligns itself to itself
that wanders away from carnivorous actions on itself
not as summoned skills profligate with mediocrity

speech within this tenor alive
being alive within prior psychic range
adverse to ejection rates from exploded stars

because human capability tends to wander Mattaesque vaccums
as base curricula
where lands morph & disintegrate & en-vigour themselves
not as warped Euclidean phonemes disfigured by blindness

alive as warped temporal equations
that fail at transformative nickel
that fail at the level of transformative strength
at evolved levels of foment

yet energies fail inside themselves
attempting prior scripts of conquest
attempting cognitive anomaly within anachronistic prisms
within exploded colonnades or towers
never the mind as insightful scoping
or Babylonian sensibility capable of superior scale as hydroxl

I feel suffused as interconnected forcefield
by which currents interact
& draw upon themselves
not as frenzy
but as latter-day osmotic perpetual with articulation
being summons to itself
not galactic sandstorm
diffuse with enigmatic pointillism

not unlike spectral voudou in Togo
not unlike twining inside itself
but as stunning electrification
renewing miraculous crucibles
not unlike the articulation issuing from stunned warlocks

this being escape
from the ensemble of a crude self-fortress
wandering untethered from oneself

flying away from carnivorous actions to oneself
spinning
according to merger with oneself
simultaneous with the self alive as primeval protraction

Quaking Interior Haven

Since existence craves its own motility
thriving on patterns of itself
never is it based on super-imposition
ignites its own concussive magnet
not as Euclidean flare
or fatigued memorabilia

it does not propound
it spirals
simultaneous with itself
every arc
every specific
effects its own range

since the universe erupts simultaneously
it fails to dwell in itself as fragment

on the surface
its resistance as dissimilarity
as ruined swans in motion
as a living field in various states of pre-competitive explosion
post-reptilian quakes
as curious synecdoche
as condensed galactic script

not human appeal
according to densely lit moral flooding

but energy according to acceleration
for instance
exploded & hurtling grammes
beyond human mortality according to accessible rates
of the human mind within the desolate grace of paradise

of course solar scale
has never been prone to link as human density
but at scale that evinces mysterious methodology
that accelerates beyond all methods of misnomer
pledging combustion to itself
I of Ankaa that assists in the change of the physical body
charged by swirling electron soils

as articulated cleansing
as cipher
as presence
simultaneous with its own belonging
not as individual crafting
but a form of feral blooming

not as indoctrinated seedling
but as precipitous concussive
as darkened maelstrom
living beyond rooted agenda
rising from a darkened neutron ravine

but there subsists a magnetism
not unlike a monster
alive as self-contained tillage of itself encrypting its own motion

endemic alchemical motion
as though its own living remained lost to itself
by means of articulated ferment
that reaches beyond the curious fate of its own appendage

as curious fate
it fails to balance its own equation
its prolific incandescence
not as boundary that burns & totters
siring the limits of disappearance
not unlike roaring elements
in the form of quaking sunsets & alums

Pluperfect Aural Fatigue

Via pluperfect aural fatigue
there exists ophthalmological aural depth
as one continues to see through speaking

because gulfs extend
one can never be certain
as to direction
that hails from continuing transparence

On Philosophical Audition

As pluperfect poltergeist it retains its aural glistening
a grammar alive
honed by ophthalmological combining

astonishing formation occurs
that extends throughout living neural registration
via inner audition
sired by ethereal humming

Living Detritus

Understanding displacement
as verbal working value
as unusual breakage
the poem appears beyond protracted struggle
beyond reinvention as demand
its evolutive element ascends as blazing
as illusive verbal utopia
above angst as scholarly research
as clinical bravura
via electrical power prone to unexpected magnification

its marrow
its bravura
extending out of nothingness
simultaneous with vulnerability
with stamina
crossing its burning plain of thought
rising via its state
of perfect electrical animation

On Stellar Origination

Not solitude that marks delimited extension
according to borders that delimit
but magnetism according to varied distance
not the qubit as synonym for land sprawl & reversal

I am thinking ignited significance that partakes of the parsecs of
    unification
of terrestrial realms as stellar unification
of every particle of thought as stellar origination
being ignited first health
where beings conjoin as aboriginal enigmas
synonymous with a motion of moons descending

On Eroded Solar Masses

Say each eroded molecular cloud
contained uncountable solar masses
not typical but density per cubic centimeter
welling up across a million years
never speaking of the highest suns through a totem of errors
but totem
taking from density no known error
alive as pattern
as irrational ascension
sans squared impalpable quanta
its implacable winds
teeming sub-flow as absentia

Imprecation as Mirage: Taroon Kampoor in Belgium

I have taken bi-pedal form as Taroon Kampoor
trembling at the cusp of nebulae & fever

to the Belgians
I remain a poltergeist
never witnessing my life as drift
never coming to consume the air I'm expected to breathe

I am Taroon in a conclave of ciphers
Taroon floating above the grass of fowl & horses

I who have accelerated the ocean inside its life base

I who have transmuted
genetic ramphotyphlops beyond its power of blindness

& because I exist as the surname Kampoor
I can never be di-invigoured
or spliced as interpretation
& assumed by stasis as immigrants' interpolation

as to stasis
as to neurosis & worry
as to imagistic phantoms
I have arrived in Belgium to convey spells

to spin from secreted toxins
so that prior phantoms uproot colonial lepers
& merge
& allow themselves gain
as haunting from Saturnian aurorae

I am sound
as living ghostly preamble
as preamble that darts
as would a feral lighting swallow

never quantified or kindled by combat
being ghost
I run amok throughout hominidae
as random cipher
as Taroon
as unserviceable quotient
spilling sparks from alien galaxies
roaming the electricity in Belgium's pointless living cradle
exposing its cells
so that they are known to the grammar that remains barbarous
    oblivion

perhaps as principle biopsy index

I repeat
I am Taroon alive by means of Saturnian aurorae
by phantom nullification
perhaps as blue or sub-orbiting species
perhaps I am gelatinous as vertebrae

according to a form of speech that issues from sub-orbiting
   migratory phantoms

I come not to ascribe or assassinate trans-regulation or intent
but to subsist by vibration
by hollow or vibrational design

yet I exist
to inculcate
to merge
to burn away the drought within thinking

I dictate my thought through seeming last resource
being power who dwells
in a seeming insular tree

therefore
I articulate through fog
through canceled iridium forges
through mundane capital as reason

there is no why or wherefore concerning my birth
no coagulated form
gathered within a freestanding mother
I being form without plasma
or fuel that gathers from electrical aurorae being visitation beyond
   ions
as if I gathered fuel from a strange Angolan hummingbird
thirsting from charred remains that float as sound
as unbrokered dust settles on Belgium

& the Belgians who advanced slaughter in the Congo
who steal extracted maggots from orphans
so as to brazenly re-sell them
as squirming mass or bread

I have alighted in parts of Antwerp Brussels Ghent
as for Flanders & the Albert Canal
they remain predisposed to infection

at times
I sense ethers wafting from Luxembourg & Germany
conversant as I am with silver birch
with Corsican Pine
with remaining deer & boar
I remain odd
not of Morocco or Arabia
not as visible house worker in Ghent
but as sorcerer who sends signals
being micro-Asiatic & leper
I am insouciant with voltage
that sometimes mimes falling by ore
or stages himself as a staggered cemetery Lion

I invade
I blaze as spectral reasoning

according to the Walloons of Flanders
I am nonbotanical

who evinces faltering as heritage
who scrawls by vapour & confoundment

therefore
I dazzle by seeming inertia
by retention of various forms of my energy perhaps an animated
    sea wall
or the energy of a leper
that dazzles as dangerous inertia
as carnivorous hesitation
as primeval hesitation according to truth

a stark & subjective rhythmos
contingent upon the side effects of sorcery not as accidentalist
or of the Lokayatas
or of the Carvaka
denying the Vedas & the soul

I remain kinetic
supernatural
not unlike a candle roaming
through perfect insects of glass

being portion as tarantula
I refuse to be understood
as strange or delimited intransigence
as dazed nomadic settling point
perjourous as regards luminosity as it bursts
from infernal infinites

& these infinites are not shaded or particulate
like subtrahends or diamonds
or triangulated thinking wells
translated from unheated suns

because I am suborder as moraine
as strange gesticular questioning
I remain in Liege
as seeming salt
as nebulous fire
seemingly transfixed by a glossary spellbound by argument
that suggests the very maintenance of God taking on the essence
    of plague
as attendant amounts of cinder

so I remain that cinder
that microscopic gust
not Brahmanical
not fazed by indifference

I being that illusive foci
that gambler
who speaks with dice in his throat
to the rational mind
my cells charged via insufficient location
as if they were microscopic gusts
torrential with liminality

this reality of spinning psychic lanterns exterminates the tamasic
with the old colonial Belgians drowned
in a curious psychic solarium

so I am seen as one who harries
tumbling & parallel with comment
knowing the nebulous has refined itself
as would broken or juggled suns
analogous to explosions or spells
between existing & non-existing
I have alighted as spell in Belgium to disrupt its platelets
to tinge its blatant animal soul

my disruption of "The Procession of the Holy Blood in Bruges"
scattering its doctrines at the University of Louvain

& why do I flutter across its moats
its coastal & interior lowlands
as if I conducted analysis
of its genuine moral psychosis

I infect their endive
their lamps
their imaginary seacoast foundations
as I balance out the Congo
as Shaman
as hummingbird
as spell

I haunt the genetic deltas of the Walloons & the Flemish

so that they'll know no rest

I remain odd inserted by dearth
as inclement writhing
as baleful phantasmagoria

facing all manner of psychic amputation they are cast as remnants
    of amputated Leopold's
self-foretold according to oceanic sums spilling from the Congo
as if I drafted judgment
making up didactic calderas
never weaning itself from objects that erupt from Saturnian flaw
being sidelong dementia brought to cryptic conclusion
by venom that flows
from swirling nebular effect
being mirage that self-surrounds its own beacon
being mirage beyond mirage
distilled from venomous slippage
not unlike lightning in ascent beyond itself like lizards that
    disappear in green sand

disappearance
didactic pneumonia
feral diagnoses

I
Taroon Kampoor
a power super-imposed
upon colonial dialectics
camouflaged by protracted conflagration

I
Taroon
beyond the pre-planned as origin
beyond explicit solar germination
pre-scripted according to unknown assignation
being telepathy by spiral

I
the oddly aligned
& so Antwerp
& Brussels
& Liege
Its populace remaining dearth as gain according to brutality that
    they've sown

all pain in the Congo not as riddle
nor self-destructive odyssey fallen into a ravine
perhaps a chiropteran flying from an invisible neutron scale
not unlike a hawk
flying from Delhi or Pompeii

perhaps in this context
I am a riotous Pelican descending from Ghana
being blood spirit
as if I had sculpted implosion

implosion sculpted from motion
as critical enclave of itself
as darkened solar arrangement

as numerical mean of optimal black vapour that shape shifts as
    blankness

I have wrought from my bearings
a ruinous levitation
my scale
problematic velocity

as if my form
failed to accrue
as a regal but darkened evil eye
being ghostly light
or tumbling Draconian jade

I
Taroon Kampoor
formed from treacherous solar ambiguity from divided cellular
    formation
from a broken form of blankness

& so my figure
ruptures into compound obscurity
etched by reflexive venom
by reflexive obscuratas

Taroon
as sigil
as errata that badgers
having fallen through the sluices of alien existence

I
who have come to emit flames from dialectical ennui
from purgatorial stammer
from strange stellar dispensation
from solar fracas
as darkened human anthropology

as singular whisper
my didactic business
pouring forth a claustrophobic nectar
not unlike fangs via hostile metamorphosis

I am the Vedas of elliptical pre-Africa
being indigenous microbe of the infinite

so on this Earth
on this continent haunted by spellbound infection
I have randomly alighted
not unlike an Angolan hummingbird
via problematic balance
along with owls & rays
& exposure to the elements

I of Vedic Africa
being an initial anima of balance
of the first minerals of auroras
purposely fraught by insular quaking

being voice from deciduous lanterns
like a sound of moons

hovering over sand

as brush fire thesis
as menace that lurks over archives
I am prone to the porous
anti-photic as riddle
like unsettled fish in curious lightning rivers

so that in Ghent
on a dark winter day
there are beings without faces
arms dark green
& specific with pollution